Bulletin Boards Should Be More Than Something To Look T5-CCG-624

By ESTHER FINTON

Illustrated By ESTHER FINTON

Copyright © Good Apple, Inc. 1979

ISBN No. 0-916456-32-3

Printing No. 123456789

GOOD APPLE, INC.
Box 299
Carthage, IL 62321

Foreword

Lucky is the teacher who spends several years teaching the same grade level. During my career, it seems as though each year brings new challenges at a new grade level. It didn't seem to matter what grade level I was teaching, but it did seem to matter how motivating my bulletin boards were. The bulletin boards in this book can easily be adapted to any elementary grade level. By altering the basic idea of each bulletin board a little, a variety of subject areas can also be incorporated. Many of the bulletin boards in this book are great for use in libraries, learning centers and media centers. One thing that all of the bulletin boards have in common is involvement. The student is invited to take part in the preparation and continuation of each bulletin board. These are not bulletin boards to sit and look at, these are bulletin boards that say, "HEY, YOU! COME AND TAKE PART. THIS BULLETIN BOARD IS FOR YOU."

For each bulletin board presented in this book you will find: 1). a purpose, 2). suggested materials for making the bulletin board, 3). worksheets for student completion, 4). additional activities. Little reference is made about color. You know what colors will look best in your classroom. Bulletin boards should be neat and attractive, but don't worry if you are not a great artist. I am not an artist. I happen to believe that children enjoy bulletin boards more if they have a hand in creating them. Student created, teacher guided bulletin boards are also more motivating. Remember, great art work is to look at. These bulletin boards are to be involved with, so dig in and enjoy.

SINCERELY,

Esther Finton

Table of Contents

Introduction

I. BACKGROUND MATERIALS

Following you will find a list of materials that can be used as a background for your bulletin boards. After you have chosen a topic, pick a background material that seems appropriate.

Cloth materials: Paper materials:

burlap   corrugated cardboard
felt   poster board
leather   construction paper
fake fur   newsprint/newspaper
a table cloth   tissue paper
interfacing   gift wrap
flannel   aluminum foil
colored cheese cloth   wallpaper
suede fabric   road maps

Use a stapler or straight pins to put up the background of your bulletin board. If you want to be able to move objects on the bulletin board easily, you can use flannel or interfacing material.

II. BORDERS

Most any of the background materials listed above could be used to create a border for your bulletin board. A combination of two different materials for background and border many times looks quite nice. Some of the bulletin boards in this book suggest you use student work, as a border. Other materials to consider for creating a border for your bulletin board include:

twisted or braided yarn or paper
heavy cord or braided cord
artificial ivy, vines, or flowers
fluted crepe paper
ball fringe
ribbon, paper flowers
snowflakes
paper doilies cut in half
seasonal cutouts

SEE EXAMPLES BELOW AND ON THE NEXT PAGE

TWISTED YARN

BaLL FRINGe

PaPeR FLoWeRS

PaPeR DOILieS CuT In HaLF

III.   LETTERING

Most any of the background and border materials
can be used for lettering. Other materials to
consider include:

yarn, rope, ribbon   cotton
seeds, twigs   glitter glued on paper
sequins, buttons   pipe cleaners
sandpaper   foam meat/produce containers
paper plates   napkins

Not all lettering needs to be exact. Use felt
pens and draw large overlapping letters freehand
and cut them out. Make letter pairs of two shades
of construction paper. Glue together slightly off-
center and it will look like a shadow. Use red
and green for Christmas or orange and black for
Halloween. These letters can also be attached to
the bulletin board with long straight pins. This
will provide dimension to your bulletin board.

Store bulletin board letters in envelopes. Write
on the outside of the envelope what the letters
say. Bulkier letters can be stored in small boxes.
The envelopes and boxes should be stored with the
appropriate bulletin board if you plan to use the
bulletin board again. It might be wise to glue a
sample letter to the outside of the envelope or
box. Larger letters can be stored in manila folders. If these containers are not available, staple
two pieces of sturdy paper together and place the
letters inside. Letters can also be stored in manila folders and stored in a file cabinet. Write
the name of the bulletin board on the tab.

IV.   Other ideas for your bulletin boards

To put up the bulletin board, use staples, pins,
map pins, or thumbtacks. If you don't want holes
in your base surface, you could tape the materials
up with double-faced tape.

If you will want to move objects, put a paper
clip under the pin or thumbtack. The picture
or object can then be placed inside the paper
clip area.

Thumbtacks can be put in the bulletin board and
magnets glued behind the pictures or objects.
Materials will stick to the thumbtack but can
also be moved rather easily by students. This
can prevent tearing.

If cloth or cloth objects are to be used on the
bulletin board you may wish to stitch small pieces
of velcro to the two objects that need to adhere
to each other.

For a dimensional effect for your bulletin board
there are several things you can do. Roll paper
for trees, branches, stems, poles and other cyl-
inder shapes. Pin or tack to the bulletin board
on the inside.

Leaves, flowers and parts of animal bodies can
be made by scoring paper. Use a pair of scissors,
crease the paper, and shape by gently squeezing.
Be careful not to cut.

Yarn and fringe can be used for dimension on your
bulletin board in many ways. It is excellent for
animal tails and manes. Yarn makes very nice human hair.

Many items for your bulletin board can be made
by weaving strips of construction paper. Several
illustrations can be found below.

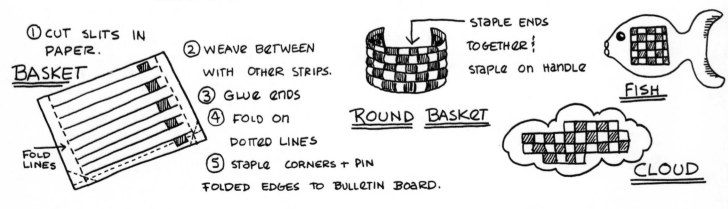

① CUT SLITS IN PAPER.
BASKET
FOLD LINES
② WEAVE BETWEEN WITH OTHER STRIPS.
③ GLUE ENDS
④ FOLD ON DOTTED LINES
⑤ STAPLE CORNERS + PIN FOLDED EDGES TO BULLETIN BOARD.

STAPLE ENDS TOGETHER; STAPLE ON HANDLE
ROUND BASKET

FISH
CLOUD

Using the overhead projector makes creating
bulletin boards much easier. Use any picture
you are wanting to enlarge, trace the picture
onto a sheet of plastic, place the sheet of
plastic on the overhead projector and move
the projector to a position where it projects
the correct size image onto your background
paper for your bulletin board. Trace over the
image with a pen or pencil that has been pro-
jected onto your background paper. Turn off the
projector and color, paint, cut out, or outline
the image you have just traced.

Zip lock bags, manila folders, large envelopes,
and shopping bags can be used to make storage
folders on your bulletin boards. Worksheets for
student use and completed work can easily be stored in this folder. A simple folder can be made by
taping or stapling together the sides of a manila
folder.

V.   Still more ideas for your bulletin board.

Many times audio-visual materials can turn a
bulletin board into a special learning area in
your classroom. Don't forget to use tape recor-
ders, record players, filmstrip projectors and
filmloop projectors in your bulletin board areas.
Materials for these machines can be used as
reference materials for your students. Worksheets can be designed to check comprehension
of the audio-visual presentations.

Store bulletin boards in large plastic bags.
Place a sheet of posterboard or cardboard inside
to keep the materials flat. Seal the bags shut
and label by writing the name of the bulletin
board on an index card and taping the card to
the outside of the bag. Another handy way to
store a bulletin board is to place the contents
between two sheets of posterboard that have been
taped or stapled together. The title of the
bulletin board can be written on the outside of
the container. Cardboard tubes are great for
storing bulletin boards. This works especially
well when a part of the bulletin board is a large
sheet of paper that you do not want to fold.
Cardboard tubes can then be stored in a box.

HOW TO MAKE YOUR OWN LETTERS BY FOLDING AND CUTTING PAPER. Using the paper cutter cut squares of paper to a desired size. Most all of the letters of the alphabet can be cut on the fold. The letters "J", "N", "Q", "S", and "Z" are the exception. It will take a little practice but you will find this an easy way to make letters for your bulletin boards.

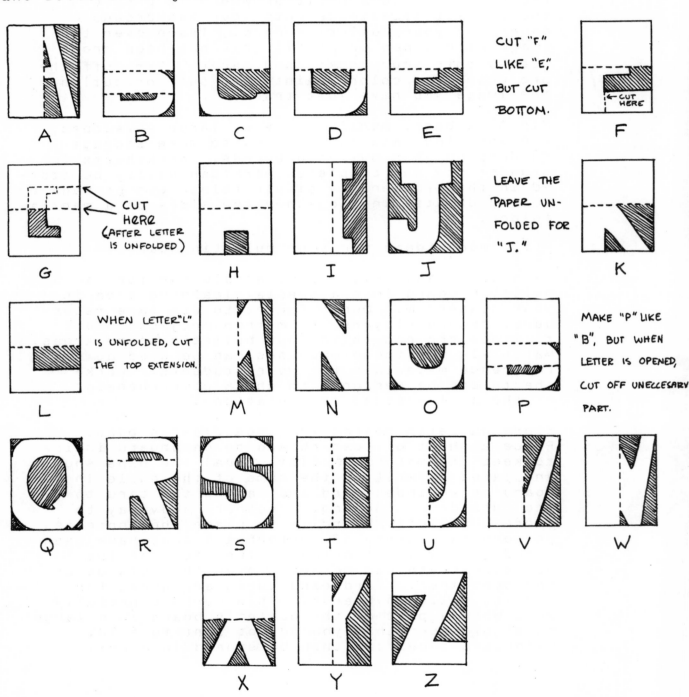

A   B   C   D   E

CUT "F"
LIKE "E",
BUT CUT
BOTTOM.

F

G

CUT
HERE
(AFTER LETTER
IS UNFOLDED)

H   I   J

LEAVE THE
PAPER UN-
FOLDED FOR
"J."

K

L

WHEN LETTER "L"
IS UNFOLDED, CUT
THE TOP EXTENSION.

M   N   O   P

MAKE "P" LIKE
"B", BUT WHEN
LETTER IS OPENED,
CUT OFF UNECESSARY
PART.

Q   R   S   T   U   V   W

X   Y   Z

WAKE UP! READ A BOOK!

PURPOSE: This bulletin board can help encourage students to read more library books. The bulletin board will also help encourage reading comprehension skills as well as creative thinking skills.

MATERIALS: The bear can be made from a piece of brown felt or from a piece of "fake fur" fabric. Use a real stocking cap and fit it on the bears head. Make the pillow and bedspread from scraps of material. Gold foil paper can be used to create a brass bed.

EXPANDED ACTIVITIES: Have each student do one of the following:
1. Make a chronological list of the major events in the story.
2. Make a list of words that describe the moods of the main character.
3. Alphabetize a list of the characters in the story.

Make a book cover for the book and write a short book review inside the front cover. Inside the back cover, draw a scene that was told in the book, but not illustrated.

SCIENCE ACTIVITY: Study animals that hibernate. Do some research. Make a list of animals that hibernate and then, after additional research, transfer the list of animals to a chart with the following headings: ANIMAL, HABITAT, FOOD, TYPE OF HIBERNATION

1

PURPOSE: Students will have the opportunity to use their imaginations and creative thinking skills to draw and write cartoons.

MATERIALS: The fence can be made of wood designed adhesive paper. Put cartoons on the fence. Have students bring the cartoons. Change the cartoons often so students will continually come to the bulletin board and read them. Make the car from poster board.

ACTIVITIES: Have each student bring some cartoons that he/she likes. Discuss what kind of cartoons there are: political, gag, and comic strip. Label the bulletin board for one type of cartoon each week and focus on that type of cartoon.

EXPANDED
  ACTIVITIES: Have the students bring comic books that are no longer wanted. Have a swap day or set up a borrowing station in your class-room.

For an art activity, students can try an art flip comic strip. Take small pages of paper and draw an object on one sheet. For example, draw a dog sleeping. On each sheet after the first sheet, have the dog begin to move by changing the picture just slightly. When the cartoon is completed staple the pages together. The student holds the picture booklet by one corner and flips the pages to make the animal move. Place a pocket on the bulletin board for students to put these in because everyone will enjoy looking at them.

2

IT'S
A
MYSTERY

Whoo

PURPOSE: This bulletin board should help motivate students to read mystery stories.

MATERIALS: Make the trash can from aluminum foil. The tent can be made of canvas or sailcloth. Make the raccoon of felt. All other objects can be made from construction paper. Across the bottom of the bulletin board tack jackets to mystery books.

EXPANDED
ACTIVITIES: Have the students use reference books including the Guinness Book of World Records to find records of mysteries of our world.

    Who disappeared, when and where?
    What human being has more teeth than anyone?
    What is the secret of the Bermuda Triangle?
    Where is the lost city of gold?
    Who are some famous writers of mystery stories?

On 3" X 5" index cards write questions. Place the questions in an envelope on the bulletin board and have students find the answers to the questions in various reference books that are available. Then, have the students report their findings to the class.

Have each student write a short mystery story. The stories can be collected and bound into a class mystery book. Make the book a part of your regular library.

MONKEY TAILS

PURPOSE: Students will gain experience in writing make believe stories.
                Creative thinking skills will be enhanced and students will
                have the opportunity to practice basic writing skills.

MATERIALS: Use yarn and a dowel stick to make the swing. The monkey
                could be made from brown and tan felt. The leaves could be
                made from various shades of green construction paper.

ACTIVITIES: Place the students stories (worksheet #1) in the spaces indi-
                cated on the trunk of the tree. Each day change the stories
                that are featured. Additional stories could be taped or tacked
                at the bottom of the bulletin board. Encourage students to go
                to the bulletin board each day and read the stories that are
                featured.

EXPANDED
  ACTIVITIES: "Don't Monkey Around" could be the title of this bulletin board.
                The students could make a dictionary of current slang terms
                that they hear around school and at home. These terms could
                be written on 3" x 5" index cards and could be filed in alpha-
                betical order. Students could also talk to their parents
                and older people and collect slang terms that are no longer
                popular.

4

Why does an elephant sit on a marshmallow?

PURPOSE:
With the help of this bulletin board students will have the opportunity to learn about codes. They will receive practice in decoding messages and will learn how to write coded messages.

MATERIALS:
The elephant can be made from felt fabric. Make the marshmallow from white felt or cotton. Glue the cotton on a piece of poster paper. The code can be made from strips of black construction paper. Use white paper for the background. You may choose to make the coffee cup from a piece of bright checked contact paper.

ACTIVITIES:
Have the students make up elephant jokes. The answer to each joke should be written in code. The jokes can be placed on one envelope at the bottom of the bulletin board and the coded answers placed in a second envelope. The jokes and the answers should be printed on 3" x 5" index cards.

EXPANDED
  ACTIVITIES:
Have the students do some research on the Morse Code. Find out who started the code, what it is used for, who uses it, and how to make a telegraph set. Have students make a telegraph set to use in the classroom.

Have students think up additional codes. Use numbers for the letters of the alphabet. An easy and fun code is to write the letters of a word in alphabetical order. So, Little Miss Muffet becomes Eilltt Imss Effmtu.

SOMETHING'S FISHY

FICTION

FACT

OPINION

PURPOSE: With the help of this bulletin board students will receive practice in determining the difference between, fact, fiction, and opinion in the written word.

MATERIALS: Make the penguin of black and white pieces of felt. Cut a slit in the mouth. Glue a mailing envelope behind the slit to hold the fact, fiction, and opinion ships. Make the fish from posterboard. Cut slits in the fins as shown in the drawing. This is where the students will place the slips that the penguin holds in his mouth. Make the water in the fishbowl from blue paper and cover with clear Saran Wrap. Use black tape to form the outline of the bowl.

ACTIVITIES: Discuss the difference between fact, fiction, and opinion or statements of judgement. A fact is something that actually happened or that is really true. An opinion is what one person thinks is true or likely to be true. Fiction is something that could not be true or did not really happen.

EXPANDED
 ACTIVITIES: Place cards in the penguin's mouth with either fact, fiction, or opinion statements on them. Have the students put these cards in the fin of the appropriate fish. In the lower corner of the bulletin board write statements on cards for students to change and place in an empty envelope on the opposite corner.

I'M A
BOOKWORM

PURPOSE: This bulletin board can help students learn to use
reference materials. The bulletin board will help students
see the need of using a library or media center to find
information. Specific skills in using the library card
catalog can be gained.

MATERIALS: The child pictured on the bulletin board can hold an actual
book jacket. Pick one that will be most appealing to your
students. The child's hair can be made of yarn. Contact
paper can be used to make the table and the book shelves.
Each student in your room can make one of the books for the
book shelf. Each child can use a favorite color of construction paper to make a cover for his/her favorite book.

ALTERNATIVE: Have the students put the name of each book
they read on the spine of a construction paper book. Use
these books to fill the library shelves on the bulletin
board.

EXPANDED
  ACTIVITIES: Make a card catalog for your library. As students read
a book, have them make the proper cards. Have students
check the card catalog before they write out a card to
eliminate duplication.

THEY HAD COURAGE

PURPOSE: This bulletin board will help students in the research of
            reference materials and acquaint them with the techniques
            of outlining.

MATERIALS: Make several of the hero cards. Change them occasionally.
            Make each card on half a sheet of poster board. Allow
            students to make additional cards for their heroes as the
            unit progresses. The lion can be made from a sheet of
            gold poster paper. His mane could be made of yarn. The
            lion's whiskers could be made from pipe cleaners.

EXPANDED
  ACTIVITIES: Have each student write a recipe for courage. These can
            be pinned to the bottom of the bulletin board area.

            Make worksheets. Title half of them, MY HERO, and the other
            half, MY HEROINE. Each student is to complete one of each.
            The student should find a picture or draw a picture of the
            person he/she chooses, and glue it on the sheet of paper
            and then write a short biography.

            Ben Franklin's Poor Richard's Almanac could be used with
            this bulletin board. Do some research on the sayings
            (proverbs) contained in the book. Have each student choose
            a saying and draw a picture to show what the saying means.

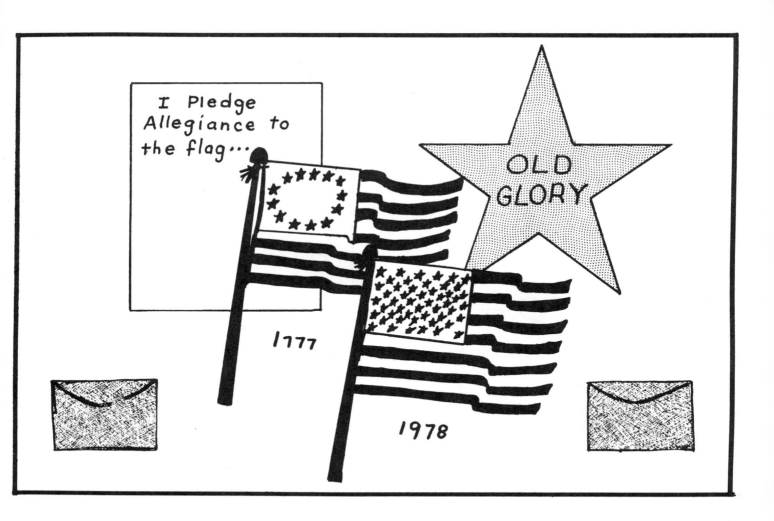

PURPOSE: With the help of this bulletin board students will learn much about our flag. History, displaying techniques, and purpose of our flag will be among the concepts presented. Students will also receive practice in using reference materials to find information about our flag.

MATERIALS: The flags on the bulletin board can be made from crepe paper or actual flags could be used. A gold tassel could be placed on each staff. The large star could be made of gold/yellow felt or of aluminum paper. Each day a different student could add another line to the Pledge of Allegiance.

EXPANDED
ACTIVITIES: Add other symbols or documents of the United States to this bulletin board from time to time. Pictures and information about the Presidents of the United States could also become part of this bulletin board.

If this bulletin board is used in February, focus on Abraham Lincoln and George Washington.

Pictures of historical places, buildings, and great Americans could also become part of this bulletin board.

Provide paper for students to draw and color flags from other nations. These flags can also be displayed. Students could also prepare a short talk about the national flag they choose to create.

Have the students use construction paper and felt tipped pens to create the flags of our fifty states.

MATCH THE OPPOSITES

EXCEPT	TIMID
BOLD	LENIENT
POSSESS	STALE
STERN	DEPRESSED
FRESH	LOSE
ELATED	INCLUDE

PURPOSE: Students will have practice matching antonyms, using them in sentences and defining them.

MATERIALS: The two characters are made from two coat hangers. The coat hangers are taped together to form the body. Use a third hanger shaped into a circle for the head. A paper plate could also be used for the head. Place a nylon stocking over the circular hanger and tie at the neck. Make a tie from a scrap of fabric and place over the knotted nylon. Add facial features and shoes cut from construction paper or felt.

EXPANDED ACTIVITIES: Use hangers and nylon stockings to make clowns for the bulletin board. Students can show emotions on the clown's faces. A word to describe the emotion can be placed on the collar or shoes of each clown. Antonyms of that word can be printed on slips of paper and attached to the body of each clown.

Worksheets can be stored in the envelopes at the bottom of the bulletin board.

On 3" x 5" index cards write one word. Be sure that each word has an antonym written on another card. Make as many cards as you have students. Each student draws a card. The student must show no one his/her word, but must find his/her antonym partner by asking questions.

A DEAR DEER

PURPOSE: Students will be able to define the word homonym and will become familiar with many words and their homonym(s).

MATERIALS: Some materials that could be used for this bulletin board are felt for the trees, bow and the deer. Felt tip markers will write and draw easily on pieces of felt. Use a piece of ball fringe for the deer's nose. You may wish to embroider the rest of the facial features onto the deer's face. You may wish to place leftover Christmas card envelopes on the trees instead of just plain white ones.

ACTIVITIES: Use worksheets #1 and #2 for practice in learning homonyms. Fold the sheets and place them in the envelopes on the bulletin board.

EXPANDED
ACTIVITIES: Use the bulletin board to study plurals. Find as many words as you can that the singular and plural are spelled alike. Place in the envelopes for students to learn. Be sure plenty of blank cards are available for students to contribute additional examples they find.

Have students write stories using the wrong homonym. The student should work with a partner and give his/her story to the partner for correction.

WHALES'
TAILS

PURPOSE: This bulletin board will provide students the opportunity to understand the possessive form of nouns. Students will have practice in working with possessive nouns.

MATERIALS: The whales can be made of kraft paper or pieces of fabric. The water can be made from different shades of blue and green construction paper. Have two openings in the waves with pockets behind them to hold the work sheets.

EXPANDED
   ACTIVITIES: Give each student a picture, for example, a snow scene or a boy playing basketball. Have the student glue the picture on a piece of paper and write ten possessives about what can be seen in the picture. The possessives should be written below the picture. Five of the possessives should be singular and five should be plural.

Use the bulletin board for a lesson in understanding possessives and contractions. Use sentences that are similar and have the students decide if the apostrophe is in a contraction or a possessive. Place the sentences on cutout fish shapes. Make two whales, one for possessives and one for the contractions. Have students place the fish under the correct whale's tail on the bulletin board.

The bulletin board can be used for a creative writing assignment. Use reference materials to find information about whales. Have each student write, "A Whale of an Adventure."

12

A GREAT BUNCH

PURPOSE: This bulletin board should develop skill in putting words in alphabetical order.

MATERIALS: The grapes, leaves and stem can be made from felt. Use pipe cleaners for the tendrils. On squares of tagboard print words. You will probably want to make several sets of words. The word cards can be taped to the grapes. The sets of words to alphabetize can vary in difficulty.

EXPANDED
ACTIVITIES: The grapes can be taken from the envelopes and pinned to the bottom of the bulletin board in alphabetical order. Students would use the envelope that contained the level of difficulty they desired. You will want to label the envelopes EASY, MEDIUM and HARD.

Instead of putting words in alphabetical order, have the students find what other things are called when they are in a group. Grapes are called a bunch. Fish are called a school. Students could match objects written on one grape to another grape that contains the group name.

There are many group names associated with human beings. Mob, audience, class, fraternity, and crowd are just a few of the possibilities. How many different ones can your students think of? Use each in a sentence to show the correct meaning.

HIT
RECORDS

REMAP
RECORD
REBUTE
RETURN
RECLINE
READ
RETRACE
REPEAT
RETAKE
REFER
REDO
REPEL

PURPOSE: Students will learn about prefixes. The bulletin board
                        can also be used to motivate vocabulary and spelling lessons.
                        Many different prefixes can be used. You may wish to try:
                        trans, dis, pre, tele, post, or anti. Each week use a new
                        prefix.

MATERIALS: The records shown on the bulletin board can be old 45 rpm
                        records that the students bring to school. A word can be
                        printed on a circle of white paper and taped over the record
                        label. Make the title, "Hit Records" large and use a record
                        for the letter "O". If you cannot find pictures of old
                        record players, you could substitute pictures of current "pop"
                        recording artists.

EXPANDED
  ACTIVITIES: Take a survey. What are the students favorite songs? Have
                        each student make a construction paper replica of their #1
                        favorite song. These could be used as a border to the bulletin
                        board. Have each student make a graph of the results. The
                        next week, do the same thing. Which songs gained in popularity?
                        Compare the two graphs.

                        Select a song with many descriptive words. Type the words
                        to the song on a master. Leave blanks where several of the
                        descriptive words should be written. Play the song. As the
                        students listen they write in the missing words. This is
                        an excellent spelling/vocabulary lesson.

FLYING GEMS

PURPOSE:	This bulletin board will help students develop a better understanding of what prefixes and suffixes are and how they affect the meanings of words. In addition this bulletin board can be used to develop student's vocabularies.
MATERIALS:	To create the butterflies, shape florist wires and cover with fabric or tissue paper. Gift wrap will also work nicely. Use a real butterfly net. Make the butterflies red and yellow for prefixes and blue and green for suffixes. The flowers and plants can be made from construction paper.
ACTIVITIES:	Use worksheets #1 and #2.
EXPANDED ACTIVITIES:	Use the bulletin board for a study of similies, as "A Cloud of Butterflies." Group many colorful butterflies by using those on completed student worksheets. Have the students illustrate other similies on these worksheets. Place completed ones on the bulletin board.

Have students take different colors of tissue paper, overlap them for variety and create additional butterflies. The butterflies could also be used to create mobiles.

Have one wing of a butterfly contain the prefix, for example, "trans" and the second wing of the butterfly contain the root word, for example, "port". Students pair wings to create butterflies that make words.

READ ALL ABOUT IT !

PURPOSE: This bulletin board will help the students learn about news- papers. The bulletin board can help students develop creative writing skills and proper skills for descriptive reporting.

MATERIALS: Use real pages from your newspaper for those shown on the bulletin board. Glue a newspaper behind the paperboy's delivery bag. This will hold activity sheets. Cut the let- ters in the title from newsprint. Outline with a black felt pen.

ACTIVITIES: Have assigned students bring news items for the bulletin board each day. Place the items on the newspapers on the bulletin board. You may wish to mount articles on black construction paper before placing on the bulletin board. Have each student give a short oral report on any article he/she places on the bulletin board.

EXPANDED
ACTIVITIES: Write a class newspaper. Have a variety of sections: jokes, puzzles, news items, sports, interviews, school news, and editorials. Have all the students participate in the publication of the newspaper. Place completed copies in the people's hands on the bulletin board when printed. Copies for the students to read can be placed in the carrier's bag.

ZIP ZIP

HEADING

GREETING

BODY

CLOSING
SIGNATURE

US
Mail

PURPOSE: This bulletin board will help students understand the parts of a friendly letter. Students will also receive practice writing friendly letters.

MATERIALS: Make the mailbag from a piece of burlap, or make from a large mailing envelope. The mailbox can be 3-D if made from poster board. Add details by using chalk on a large sheet of poster paper.

EXPANDED
ACTIVITIES: Research the early way of delivering mail. Learn about the pony express, the first ways of delivering the mail, the rising costs of mailing letters, the length of time required to deliver mail and other postal regulations.

Invite your postmaster or assistant postmaster to class to give a talk. Take the students to the post office.

Write invitations to a party for parents or for members of another class. Students can plan the cost of the party and plan for the food and games. Don't forget decorations. Make a list of proper manners and post in the room.

HAVE YOU LOOKED IN THE YELLOW PAGES

Physicians & Surgeons

M. D.

James, Robert T.
Totem Street
Crest, IL
783-9959

PHOTOGRAPHER

Bob's Studio
4th and Clay
Starr, IL

756 - 8339

Pharmacy
Rx
Johnson Drugs

605 Main
735-7708

PLUMBING
CONTRACTORS
Bill's Plbg & Htg.

Bates
705 - 3368

PURPOSE: This bulletin board will help the students to learn more about the telephone and how to use it correctly. The bulletin board will also help teach the prefix tele.

MATERIALS: Use yellow paper for the pages of the telephone book. A cord can be used for the telephone. Use yarn for the hair of the person using the telephone. Fabric can be used for the lady's dress. Place the cover of a real telephone book in the lady's hand.

ACTIVITIES: Have the students practice looking up names in the yellow pages of the telephone book. Your local phone company may be happy to furnish your class with several copies of your local phone book. Also use the dictionary to study the prefix "tele". How many words can you find that begin "tele"? What do those words mean?

EXPANDED
ACTIVITIES: Have the students learn the correct way to answer the telephone and to take messages. The students can practice calling each other and answering the phone. Messages can be given and recorded if the students are paired. Have students make a list of proper phone manners. Write these on cards and place on the bulletin board.

Cut pictures of people from magazines. The people should be talking on the telephone. Make a collage of these pictures.

NEATO FAVORITES

PURPOSE: This bulletin board should allow students to develop a more positive self-concept. It should also allow students to become more aware of their own feelings as well as the feelings of their classmates.

MATERIALS: Real objects or pictures of objects can be placed on the strip of film. A small reel of film can be placed in the boy's hand. Borrow one from the library or from the audio-visual person at your school. Change the objects on the film often. You might wish to allow each student in your class to bring something to be placed on the strip of film.

ACTIVITIES: Have each child make a "Who Helps Me Each Day" book. Each student's book can be bound separately or all books can be bound into one book for the entire class to enjoy. Each book may be a different length. Class discussions will help each child to expand his/her book. Each page in the book should name or show the picture of someone who helps the child. The page should also contain a few sentences telling how that person helps.

EXPANDED
  ACTIVITIES: Keep a calendar of special events in the classroom. Put student birthdays, holidays, special occasions, piano recitals, ball games, etc. on the special events calendar. This calendar can help in learning basic skills about the calendar as well as help students see and relate to the specialness of each member of the class.

DIRECTIONS: Use these four positive notes as incentive to your students to do good work. You can fill in the blank areas to best express your feelings.

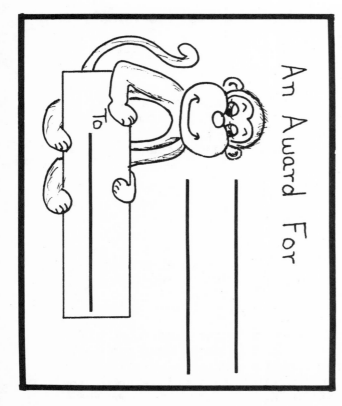

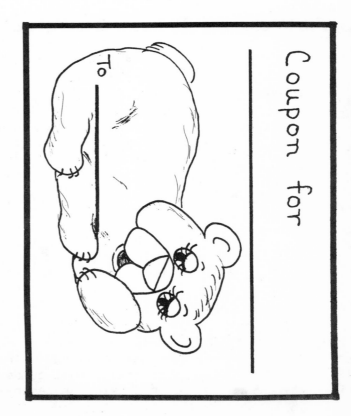

INSTRUCTIONS: Write a report about one of your favorite books. Place your report in the envelope on the bulletin board. You may write several reports if you wish.

_____

_____

_____

_____

_____

_____

_____

When you have finished your report, you may read any of the reports in the folder.

INSTRUCTIONS: Read eight library books of your choice. List each book that you read on one of the jars. When you finish turn your list in for a sweet treat.

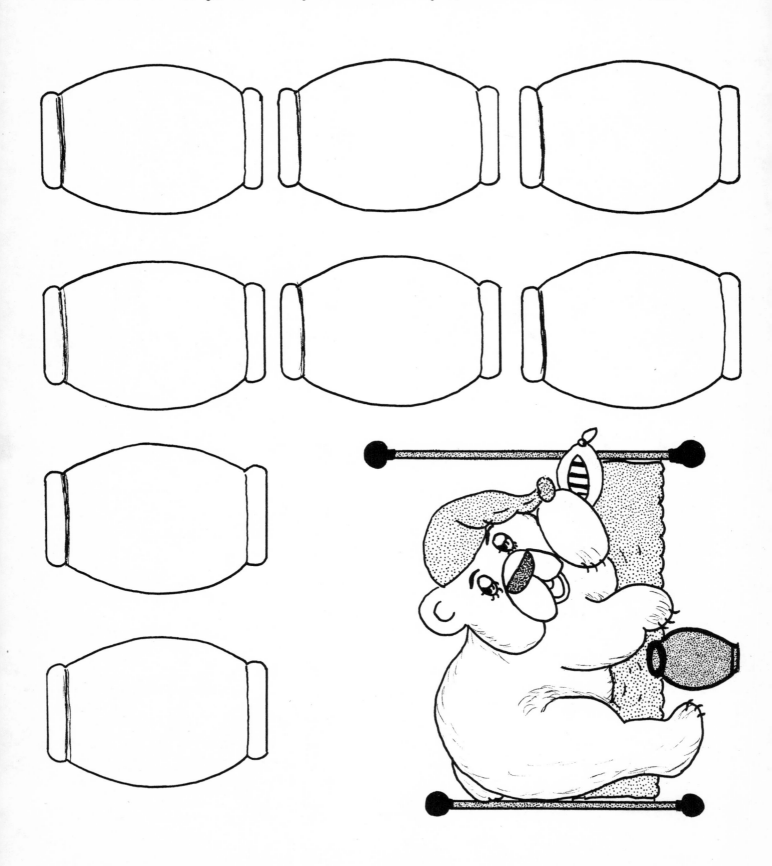

INSTRUCTIONS: Use this page to draw your favorite cartoon character. Write a caption for your picture. Be sure to sign your name as all cartoonists do.

INSTRUCTIONS: Match the name of the comic strip to its creator.

A. Chic Young

B. Dr. Seuss

C. Walter Kelly

D. Al Capp

E. George McManus

F. Charles Schulz

G. Jerry Siegel

H. Walt Disney

I. Chester Gould

J. Harry Fisher

K. Marjorie Buell

L. Robert Ripley

_____ Mickey Mouse

_____ Little Lulu

_____ Blondie

_____ Dick Tracy

_____ Superman

_____ Pogo

_____ Believe it or Not

_____ Cat in the Hat

_____ Peanuts

_____ Bringing Up Father

_____ Li'l Abner

_____ Mutt and Jeff

Can you add some more of your favorites?

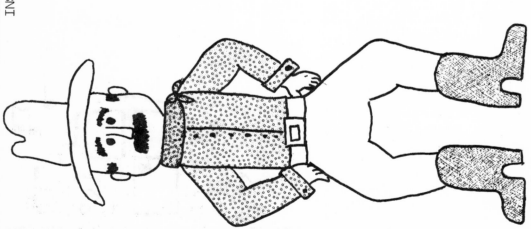

"Sir, I want to buy a horse. Everyone says I'd be a good cowboy."

INSTRUCTIONS: Read a mystery book and fill in this sheet. Draw a picture pertaining to the book you read, in the upper right-hand corner. When completed turn your sheet in to the teacher. It will become part of a guide for all students in the room. The guide will help the students to pick a book they will enjoy reading.

MY MYSTERY

_____

Name of Book

_____

Author

_____

Main characters in the story include:

_____

_____

_____

_____

_____

And here is some information about the

story._____

_____

_____

_____

_____

_____

_____

_____

_____

_____

_____

Report made by _____

INSTRUCTIONS: See if you can find something mysterious or odd about these animals.

GIRAFFE _____

SKUNK _____

GORILLA _____

TENREC _____

KODIAC BEAR _____

HUMMINGBIRD _____

PARROT _____

BABOON _____

FOX _____

CHEETAH _____

ANACONDA _____

SPERM WHALE _____

JAVIAN RHINO _____

AFRICAN BULL
ELEPHANT _____

MANDRILL OF
WEST AFRICA _____

SAVI'S WHITE
TOOTH PYGMY
SHREW _____

I sound like a baby
when I cry!

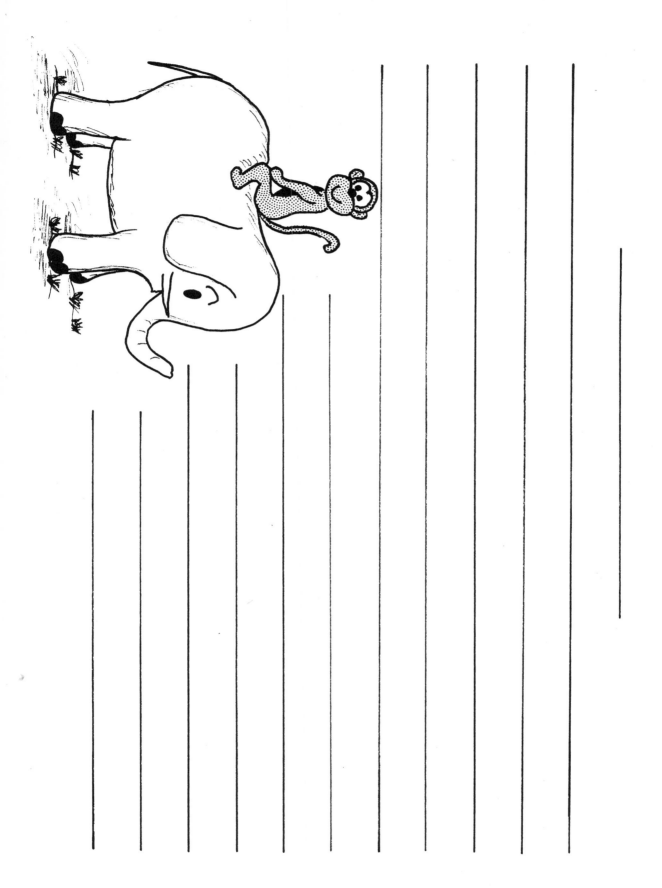

27

INSTRUCTIONS: Read the caption under each picture. Find the "TALL TALES". Color the pictures that contain "TALL TALES" captions. Write new captions for these captions.

An elephant has five toes. It can hear well and sees even better.

A pig has cloven hoofs and his bristles are made into brushes.

Some people call puppies, "Fido". Fido means "faithful one" in Latin.

A mouse is a rodent and is a member of the rat family.

Fish breathe air through gills and they all have scales.

All rabbits are called hares.

INSTRUCTIONS: Decode the answer to the question on the bulletin board by using the Morse Code . Place the answer on the lines at the bottom of the page. The bottom half of the page can then be cut off and used for a cover to a book of elephant jokes that you and your friends think up, find, and illustrate.

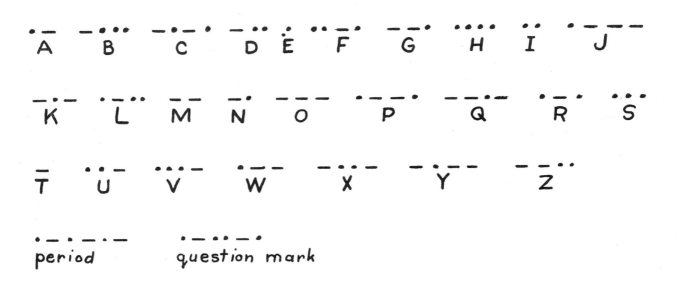

A	B	C	D	E	F	G	H	I	J
·–	–···	–·–·	–··	·	··–·	––·	····	··	·––

K	L	M	N	O	P	Q	R	S
–·–	·–··	––	–·	–––	·––·	––·–	·–·	···

T	U	V	W	X	Y	Z
–	··–	···–	·––	–··–	–·––	––··

·–·–·– period   ··––·· question mark

29

INSTRUCTIONS: Break the code. Write the answer. Draw an illustration of the joke. Be sure to make your drawing colorful.

Why did the elephant wear a green suit?

— — —   •••• ••   — ••• ••   — — •

•••• ••   — • — — •   — • • ••   — • — •

— • • • —   •   •   — •• — •

INSTRUCTIONS: Color the fish the correct color. Red, if the statement is fact; blue, if the statement is fiction;and yellow, if the statement is an opinion. The statements should then be changed by you so that each is a fact, or opinion.

FISH TASTE GOOD.

"I'M HUNGRY!", SAID THE LITTLE PENGUIN.

PENGUINS EAT FISH.

PENGUINS ARE THE CUTEST OF ALL ANIMALS.

"PLEASE DON'T EAT ME!", SAID THE FISH.

A FISH HAS GILLS.

INSTRUCTIONS: Write a story about the picture. In your story use at least two facts, two statements of judgement and two events that are fictitious.

INSTRUCTIONS: Use the encyclopedias to find the following information. Write your findings in the appropriate spaces.

Place the numbers and letters of the volumes of the encyclopedias you used on the spines of the books below. Draw more books if you need to.

TRY THESE!

REFERENCE BOOKS

Now inch along to these !

Use your encyclopedias to find cross-references for these topics

WHALES SHARKS _____ _____ _____

CLINKER _____ _____ _____

STARS AND BARS _____ _____ _____

DERMIS _____ _____ _____

POLLIWOGS _____ _____ _____

NUTRIA _____ _____ _____

LITTLE AMERICA _____ _____ _____

FOX INDIANS _____ _____ _____

GOAT ISLAND _____ _____ _____

BOOKBINDING _____ _____ _____

HIPPOCAMPUS _____ _____ _____

DIHEDRAL WINDS _____ _____ _____

CONY _____ _____ _____

AMUSEMENT PARKS _____ _____ _____

GREAT BRITISH POETS _____ _____ _____

CLASSICAL MUSIC _____ _____ _____

BALLOONS _____ _____ _____

INSTRUCTIONS: In what general classification would you find books listed on this activity sheet? Go to the library (school or community), use the Dewey decimal system to find the classification and the call number.

000 – 099 General Information	500 – 599 Science
100 – 199 Philosophy	600 – 699 Technology
200 – 299 Religion	700 – 799 Fine Arts
300 – 399 Social Sciences	800 – 899 Literature
400 – 499 Languages	900 – 999 History

1. A book of Bible prophets _____

2. How to speak German _____

3. The first dictionary for students _____

4. A history of the Incas _____

5. Trees of the Northwest _____

6. Famous paintings of the 1900's _____

7. Songs of Johann Sebastian Bach _____

8. How to take care of a cold _____

9. Haiku poetry _____

10. The churches of Rome _____

11. Baseball rules _____

12. The Revolutionary War _____

13. The first space flight _____

14. The story of Christmas _____

15. My philosophy of life _____

16. How microwave ovens work _____

17. The leading exports of Thailand _____

18. Hibernation habits of bears _____

INSTRUCTIONS: Do some research on three of the people listed on the bulletin board. Make an outline of some phase of each person's life. Then write two or three paragraphs about the life of one of the three people you chose.

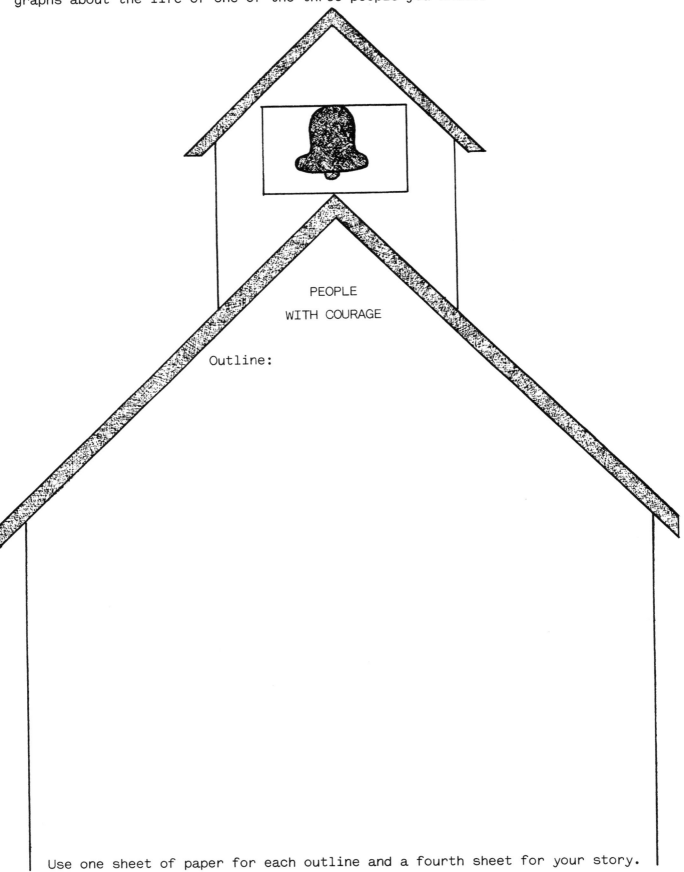

PEOPLE

WITH COURAGE

Outline:

Use one sheet of paper for each outline and a fourth sheet for your story.

INSTRUCTIONS: Find the words given in the list in the word search puzzle. The words will be found vertically, horizontally, or diagonally, forward or backward in the puzzle. Circle each word as you find it.

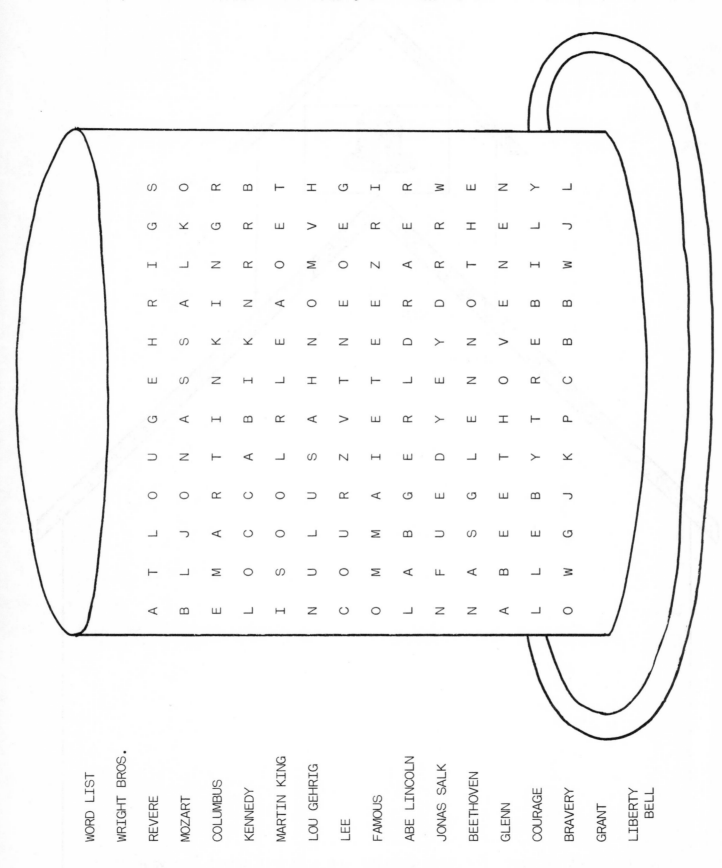

WORD LIST

WRIGHT BROS.
REVERE
MOZART
COLUMBUS
KENNEDY
MARTIN KING
LOU GEHRIG
LEE
FAMOUS
ABE LINCOLN
JONAS SALK
BEETHOVEN
GLENN
COURAGE
BRAVERY
GRANT
LIBERTY BELL

36

INSTRUCTIONS: On this worksheet draw the state flag of the state that was assigned to you. All fifty flags will be used as part of a classroom display, so do a good job.

INSTRUCTIONS: Under each star, explain what each word/group of words inside the star means. Definitions can be written on the back of this sheet. Two stars are blank. You provide something for inside the star and then its meaning.

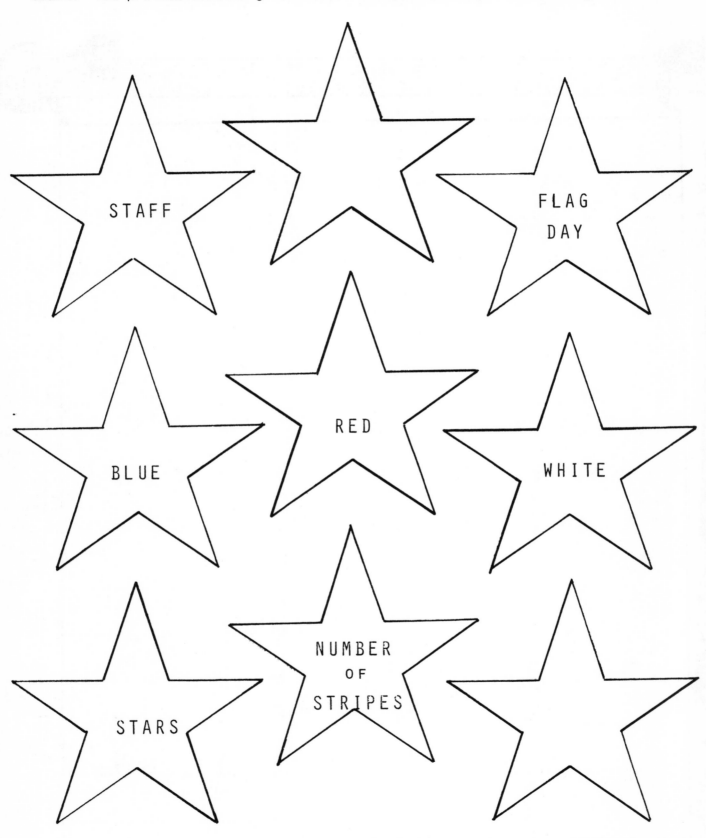

INSTRUCTIONS: Have the students write words under the two characters to tell how the character feels. Use the words from the bulletin board as well as some additional words the students discover.

INSTRUCTIONS: For each picture below, write how it makes you feel. On the second line, write a word that is opposite of that feeling. For example, delicious and distasteful. You may use a thesaurus, if you wish, so you can discover some really good words to use.

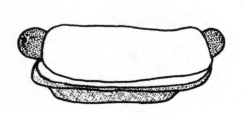

_____   _____   _____   _____

_____   _____   _____   _____

_____   _____   _____   _____

INSTRUCTIONS: Students should rewrite the following story using the correct homonyms.

THE LITTLE DEAR

Once upon a thyme, a dear was living in a huge forest. He lived with his Ant Merry and Uncle Herald Dear. He was usually a very happy, gleeful dear, but he had become very sad. He wanted too bye his ant a knew fir coat, but he didn't have won scent two his name. Little dear decided to look four a job and went to sea the grate big elephant who owned a tree removal business. He worked every knight for Mr. Elephant. His job was two lite up the forest buy shining his knows sew bright that Mr. Elephant could work late in the knight.

Ant Merry Dear was delighted with her gift even though Little Dear forgot to rap her gnu fir coat.

_____

_____

_____

_____

_____

_____

_____

INSTRUCTIONS: Draw a picture of each homonym listed on this page. Write the other homonym below the picture. If you have room think up some more.

OAR

ANT

CENT

URN

HARE

TOE

SHOE

shoo

PAWS

pause

WHALES' TAIL

INSTRUCTIONS: Place all singular possessives on the whale.

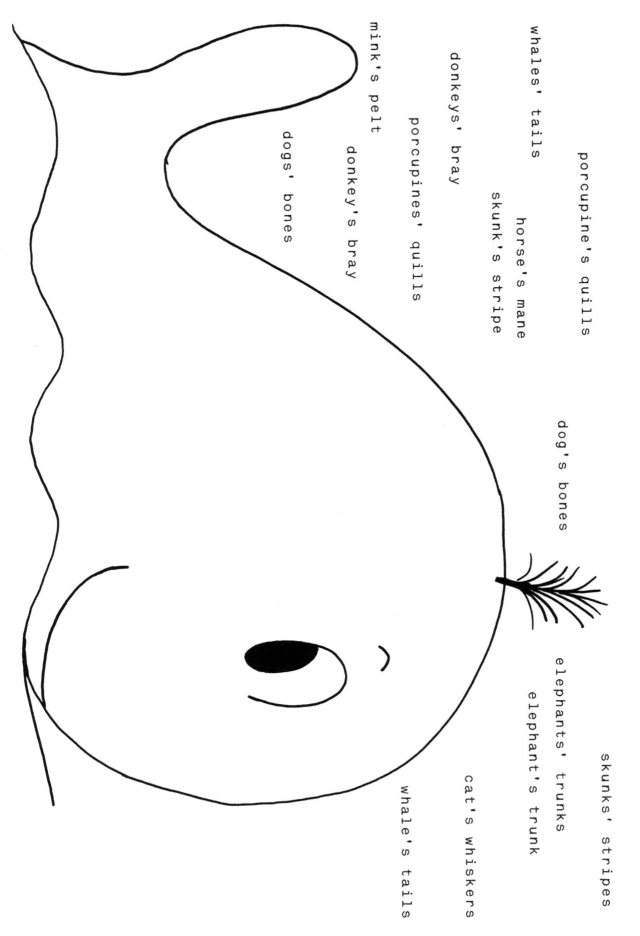

porcupine's quills

whales' tails

donkeys' bray

mink's pelt

horse's mane

skunk's stripe

porcupines' quills

donkey's bray

dogs' bones

dog's bones

skunks' stripes

elephants' trunks

elephant's trunk

cat's whiskers

whale's tails

INSTRUCTIONS: For each picture, write a sentence with a possessive about the picture. Below it write a sentence with the
opposite form of the possessive. If singular tail on the pig,
write the plural the second time.

INSTRUCTIONS: Place the first names of some of your friends on the grapes. Then, number the grapes so your friends are in alphabetical order. Finally, write your friend's names in the column that is provided.

45

INSTRUCTIONS: Place the words from the bulletin board in the grapes on this worksheet. Number the grapes 1 – 20 and then be sure the words are placed in alphabetical order.

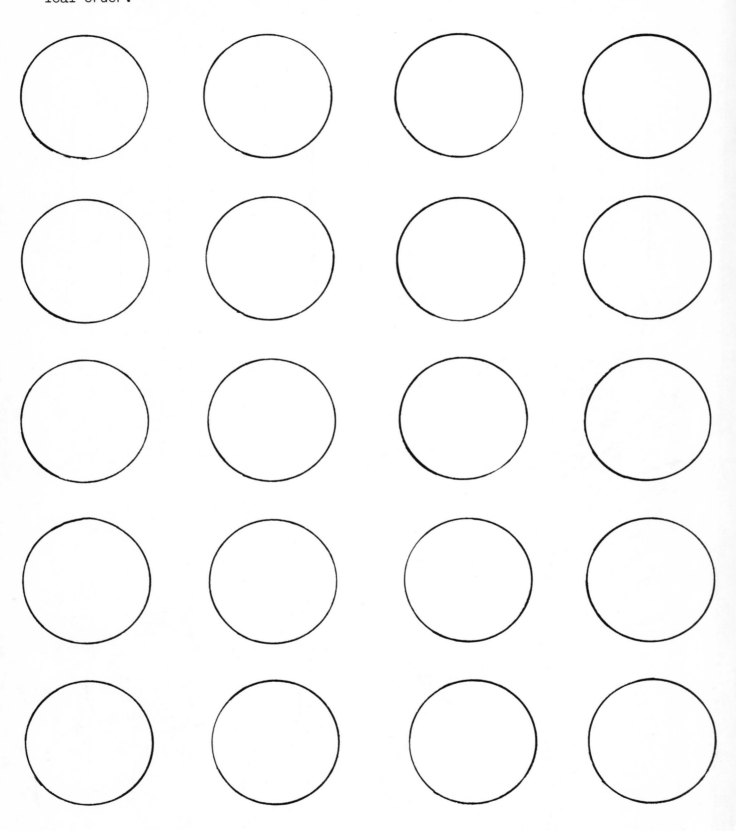

INSTRUCTIONS: Write the words, from the records on the bulletin board, on the records on this page. Color the record label blue if the word has a prefix. Color the label green if the word does not have a prefix. Under each record, write another word that has the prefix. You may have to use reference materials to find words.

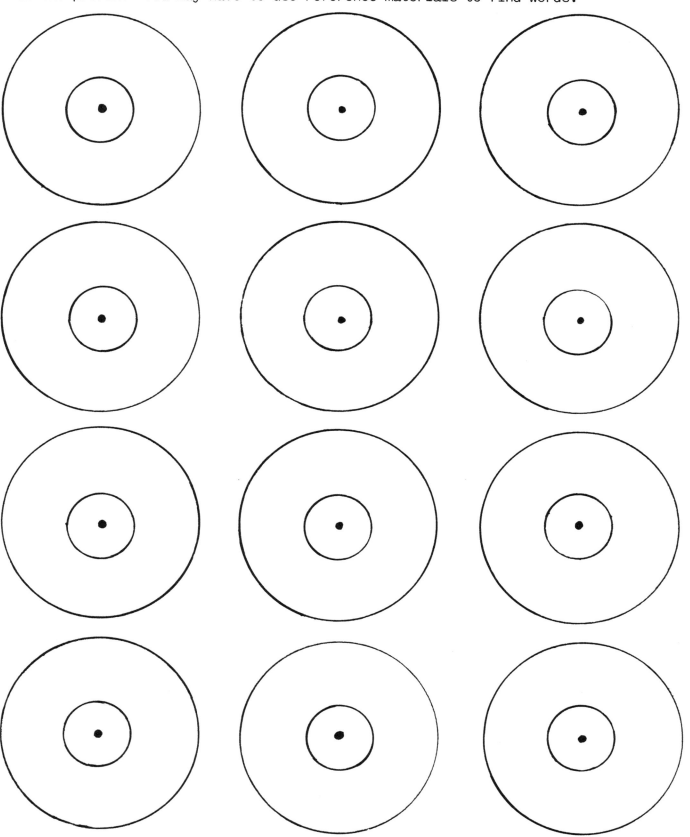

INSTRUCTIONS: Use your dictionary to help you complete this worksheet. Place some words that have "RE" as a prefix on the lines of the record. On the back of this sheet write the definitions of each word. Give this page to a friend. Can he/she define the words you listed?

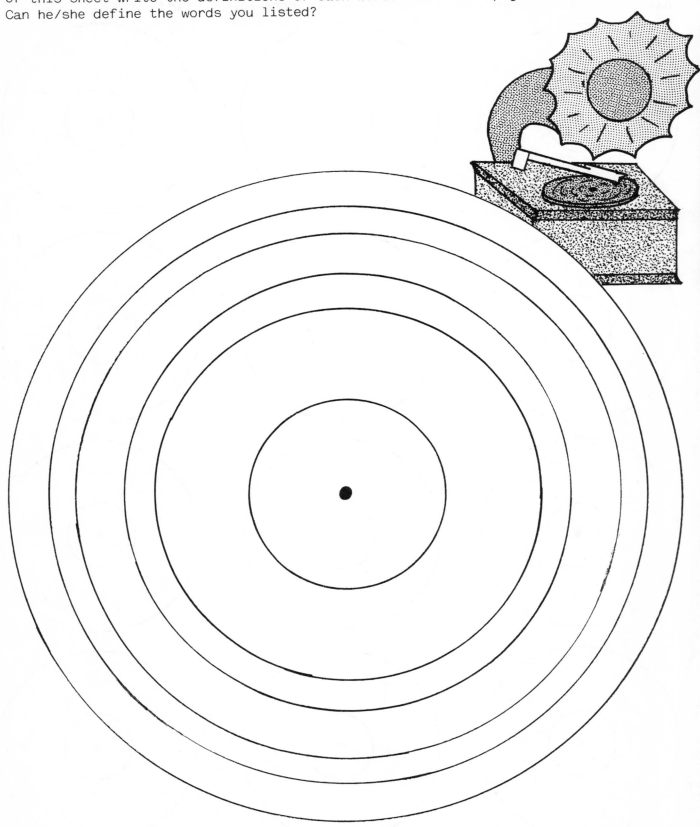

INSTRUCTIONS: Find words that have the suffix "LY". Put them on the left wing of the butterfly. Write words with the suffix "FUL" on the right wing. How many words can you find for each wing? After grading your paper and coloring your butterfly, hang it as part of the border to the bulletin board.

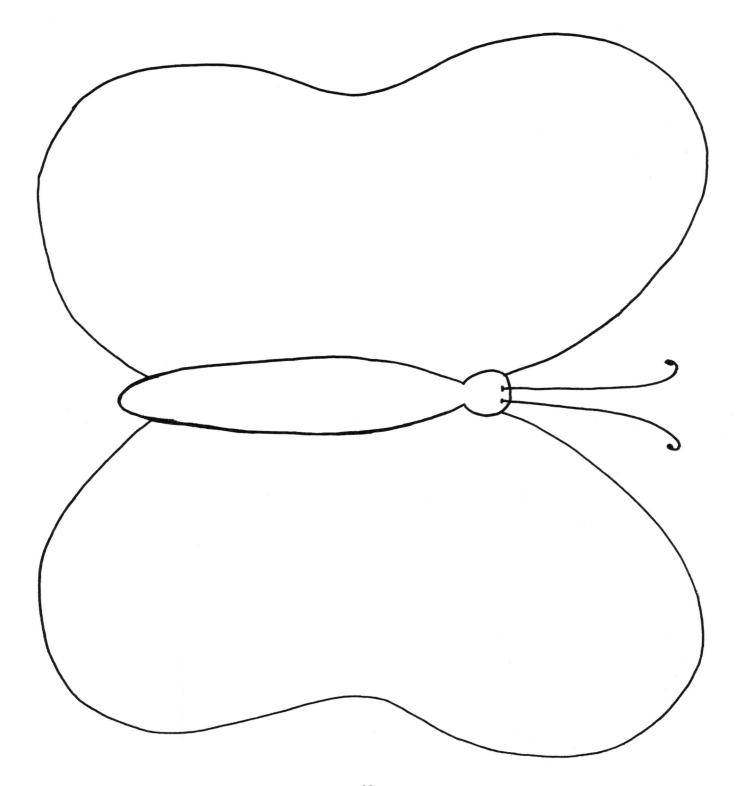

INSTRUCTIONS: Color the butterflies that have prefixes red and yellow. Color the butterflies that have suffixes blue and orange. After the pages are graded, cut out the butterflies and use them for the border of the bulletin board.

SUCCESSFUL

PEACEABLE

DISAPPEAR

TRANSPORT

UNKIND

IMPOSSIBLE

SOUTHWARD

CARRIER

NEAREST

DISLOYAL

QUICKLY

INSTRUCTIONS: Take a survey. Ask 10 people what part of the paper they read first. Record your results. Have the class compile statistics from the findings. The last two spaces can be filled in with other sections of the paper.

WHAT PART OF THE NEWSPAPER DO YOU READ FIRST?

SPORTS

CARTOONS

ELECTIONS RETURNS

HEADLINES

_____

_____

_____

_____

_____

_____

EDITORIALS

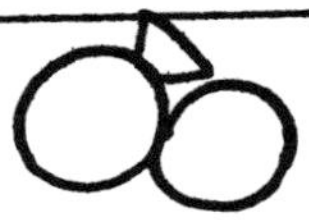

SOCIETY

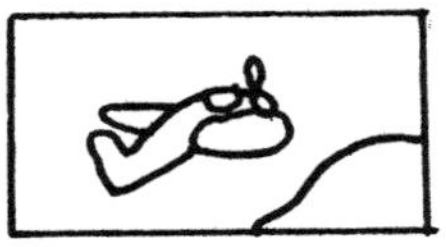

PICTURES - CAPTIONS

_____

_____

_____

_____

_____

_____

WANT ADS

_____

_____

_____

_____

_____

_____

INSTRUCTIONS: You are a reporter for the school newspaper. You just watched a spaceship land in the middle of the ball diamond. Write an article about what you saw.

INSTRUCTIONS: Have fun working this crossword puzzle.

ACROSS

3. Part of the letter that says
   hello. (plural)

5. It is part of the heading.
   It tells what today is.

7. This is placed after the name
   of the state in the heading.

8. This is used in the greeting
   before a person's name.

DOWN

1. This is placed after an ab-
   breviation.

2. These are placed in the upper
   right-hand corner of a letter.

4. This is your name.

6. This is the main part of a
   letter.

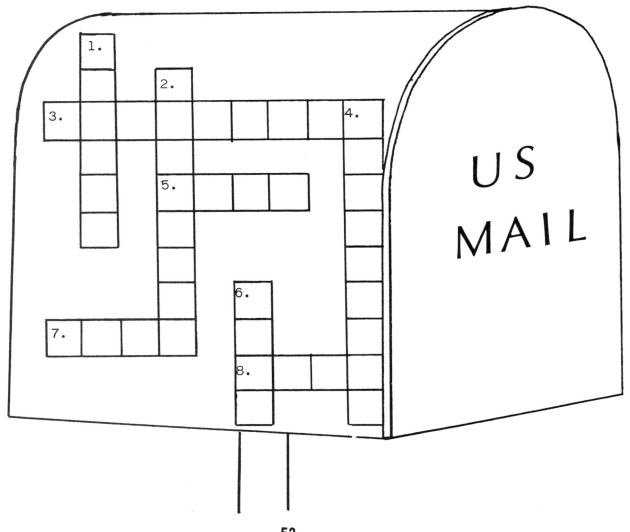

INSTRUCTIONS: After studying the parts of a letter on the bulletin board label
the parts of the letter on this page. Next, turn this page over and write a
letter to a friend. Be sure your letter is correctly written.

1355 Elm St.
Carthage, Ll. 62321
May 7, 1979

Dear Billy,
    We want you to come
visit us at our farm this
weekend. We will pick you
up at four o'clock Friday.

                    Love,
                    Aunt Nell

INSTRUCTIONS: Look up emergency numbers in the yellow pages of the telephone
directory of your city or area. List the numbers in alphabetical order on
the page of the telephone directory on this page. Don't forget the police, the
ambulance, the fire department, and the doctor. Design a symbol for each
number you place in your emergency directory.

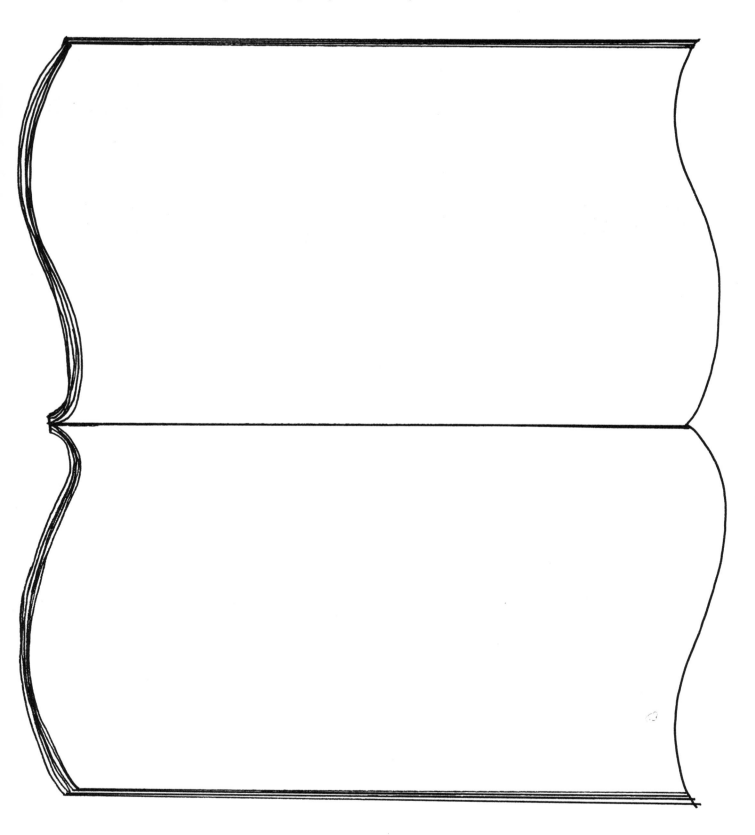

INSTRUCTIONS: Under each set of eyes, write a word that tells how that set of eyes makes you feel. If you wish, you may use reference books to help you find the words you want to use to describe the various eyes. Then, complete the bottom portion of the worksheet.

HOW DO WE FEEL?

_____ _____ _____ _____

_____ _____ _____ _____

..... AND THIS IS WHAT MAKES ME.........

ANGRY _____

JEALOUS _____

EMBARRASSED _____

JUBILANT _____

CONTENTED _____

SELF-CONSCIOUS _____

EAGER _____

ELATED _____

POPULAR _____

GRUMPY _____

ENVIOUS _____

TIRED _____